THE POWER
OF
VISUALIZATION
A Quick Guide

Yoselem G. Pintos

CONTENTS

PREFACE

In this book, you will find successful techniques to harness the subconscious mind with visualizations.

Brain studies now reveal that thoughts produce mental instructions as actions.

You will learn the visualization techniques and to activate your creative powers.

All that you wish for is within you. You just need to learn how to reprogram yourself, and once you learn how to put the power of visualization to work, you will be able to create whatever you desire.

THE POWER OF VISUALIZATION.

"Logic will get you from A to B. Imagination will take you everywhere." ...
Albert Einstein

They are hidden quantum laws of the universe that you can use to attract what you want in life.

Many goals can be achieved through visualization, and it is a relatively simple technique to undertake.

You just need to take the time on a regular basis to imagine things you want to happen in your life as if they have already come to pass. You can combat pesky, negative thoughts by replacing them with visions of what you desire to create.

The more detailed you make your visualizations, the more powerful they will be.

Begin by picturing what you want in your mind's eye. Once you have achieved this step, extend your creative visualizations to include sounds, smells, tastes, and feelings associated with the object or situation you desire.

What is what you want? What do you really want? You can easily attract what you want, because everything and all possible realities already exists. We live in a world of infinite realities. By focusing on a specific outcomes, your subconscious mind can make that reality.

TIME DOESN'T EXISTS.

"The distinction between the past, present and future is only a stubbornly persistent illusion." Albert Einstein

Forget about the time, let it go. Albert Einstein showed us that time doesn't exist. We live in a continuously present. Everything is pure energy outside of the third dimensional reality; in different speeds, and vibrations.

Think of a specific incident, or circumstance, if you achieve what you want. Take a split second of what you want and repeat that sequence in your mind; adapting your subconscious mind and re-imaging things the way you want. You have free will, and the ability to think whatever you want to think.

You get to entertain what you want in your consciousness, by re-image what you want to change with colors, erasing what you don't want, and replace it and putting your feelings in what you really want.

When you can start managing the way you're feeling, and getting emotionally involved in the way you want it; then, you are changing your patterns, to bring your expectations to reality.

RE IMAGING YOUR SUBCONSCIOUS MIND.

"Begin noticing and being careful about keeping your imagination free of thoughts that you do not wish to materialize. Instead, initiate a practice of filling your creative thoughts to overflow with ideas and wishes that you fully intend to manifest. Honor your imaginings regardless of others seeing them as crazy or impossible." Wayne Dyer

1Get emotional involved with that level of reality to attract what you want. You have to start re-imagining to attract what you want easily.

When you can start to managing the way you deal with your own feelings, you are regenerating those feelings, getting new ideas, and changing your patterns.
See yourself as a person that attracts abundance. Recreate your experiences in your mind. Pretend that you already attracting what you want in life. Be in that specific emotional experience. The goal is to recreate that experience, in your mind; reprogramming your subconscious mind, having that recreating force.

By the quantum law of the universe, there are unexplainable energies of realities from different perspectives. So put your energy and frequency in the reality and perspective that you really want it to be.

YOUR INNER WORLD.

"So what do you want? Does what happens inside show on the outside? There is such a great fire in one's soul, and yet nobody ever comes to warm themselves there, and passersby see nothing but a little smoke coming from the top of the chimney, and go on their way."
Vincent van Gogh, The Letters of Vincent van Gogh

You need to decide, what is what you really want; write it down in a piece of paper, and literally say no to anything that is not in alignment of what you want, or who you want to be, or accomplish in life.

Make a plan. Write five things that you want to do everyday. This practice will cause to move the creative energy forward. Work on it with dedication, put your mind, soul and heart on it. Take action! This is your time!

Work for it every single day no matter what.

See it, aloud in your eyes of what you want to see. Relinquish what your eyes are telling you. Close your eyes, and imagine the place you are, imagine where you really want to be, how you want to be. Imagine the room you want to be in. Feel what wealth feels like, what abundance feels like, what health feels like, what love feels like. Feel successful, What it feels to have the job you love? See this job, see this amazing manifestation in your body. What does it feels in your body?

Your subconscious is a feeling mind, your rational mind that controls ninety five percent of your life. You have to feel the essence of it. Feel the essence of what you want.

No one can take away your inner world, you need to stop telling yourself that it's impossible, because you are not vibrating in the frequency and essence of what you want.

The universe is your best friend, is the higher intelligence, and it's communicating with you.

BE AWARE OF THE BLESSINGS.

"My life has been a blessing. I'm grateful for everything I do have and the places I'm going and the things I've seen." Leah LaBelle

Move into an energy of appreciation. Keep been grateful for you already daily blessings, and the blessings you want to receive, see if you can exhilarate that energy field.

Be thankful for the roof over your head, food, water, clothing, your senses, your feelings, and all the beautiful universe and nature that God created for you to enjoy.

When you are moving into a positive energy and you are grateful for your daily small blessings; the awareness of these blessings, creates and connect to that energy even more, and this creates an amazing vibe that can attract in speed of light more blessings into your life.

Feel that you are on the right track Take advantage of the opportunities, feel that you are following the right energies, the right path; that you are aligned with everything and everything is aligned with you.

SYNCHRONIZING YOUR ENERGIES.

"Passion is energy. Feel the power that comes from focusing on what excites you." Oprah Winfrey

When you switch and synchronize your energies in the frequencies of what you already want, everything is about change, be aware that changes are coming, and to make the changes necessary to get into what you want.

Do not feel afraid of the changes. Feel your divine connection with the universe and all what it is. You are divined guided to fulfill your purposes and goals in life.

You have what it takes to make your life successful in all ways, all you have to do is to synchronize your emotions and feelings with the energy field of what you want.

Feeling that energy of what you want in your in your guts, in your veins, and knowing that you already have it; it's true awakening on your spiritual realm, on your true self, and in who you really are. You are awakening your spirit, to receive the blessings that you have the right to receive.

SIGNS THAT YOUR SPIRIT IS AWAKENING.

"You have to grow from the inside out. None can teach you, none can make you spiritual. There is no other teacher but your own soul." – Swami Vivekananda

When your spirit is awakening you're becoming to have harmony and feel your emotional body.

You starting to recognize how negativity reacts in your body. You have the knowledge, and feel that you need to get away from toxicity. Recognizing, taking boundaries of what feels good and what feels bad.

You feel more in alignment with your vibrations, and what people and places and events are offering.

You begin feeling a divine purpose in your life, that is filling you with a deeper passion and alignment of what is going through you. This inner calling, is asking you something bigger, to chase those dreams and become more independent.

You know you have to take risks for your dreams, and you let go of your fears, having a deeper knowing that the universe supports you.

Your relationship with the universe becomes extremely powerful, chasing your dreams in deeper desires. Sharing your wisdom and experiences to empower your life with good feelings and actions.

You have this deep desire to do something, you are reaching to the universe to support you. This is how you know you really are in your way to make changes in your life.

When you continuously step into your voice and power, when you align with this spiritual connection with the universe, and you know that the universe have your back.

RECOGNIZING THE SIGNS OF SPIRITUALITY.

You have to grow from the inside out. None can teach you, none can make you spiritual. There is no other teacher but your own soul. – Swami Vivekananda

What is being Spiritual?

Have you ever feel that you don't belong in this world, that there is more into it? That you want to see changes and you are not happy with the success you are developing in your spiritual life?

You have tried so hard to fit into any religion, but no one makes you feel full, satisfied and wholly connected to your true self. So then you have created your own religion or even become agnostic or atheist for a while.

Well, while this seems to be bad news, are actually very good ones!

These are signs that you are seeking your true self, your higher self, the purpose of your life, looking for your spiritual home.

- You know there is something more deep arranged to everything around you.
- You feel connected to every single source of living.
- You feel alive, you know that God is something more powerful and wonderful than the one that we know in the Bible.
- You feel the discrepancies in your heart, but you are afraid to let society know your true feelings, fearing the

possible rejections, so you create your beautiful inner world in your own true, called your own religion.

- You create your own rules, your own truth, and you feel very good about it, you feel at home, and this is what you want to believe, it's you connected to the universe with amazing learning everyday experiences.
- You start seeing things in a different perspective than anyone else.
- You see value in simple things, you appreciate life, and you can feel the essence of nature connected to your body, to your soul, to your mind.
- You love to be in contact with nature and you are part of it.
- You start to understand that you are in perfect time, in the perfect place at the perfect situation to synchronize and vibrate with the rest of the world in existence.
- You start to feel love for everything and understand how life goes. You feel that you are divined guided by spirit and light frequencies.
- You feel that your spiritual awakening helps the world to become a better place to live, bringing light, love, and hope to this world.
- You feel this beautiful connection of your soul with the rest of the existence, feeling proud and part of the creation, and know now that your life has a meaning and everything has a purpose.
- You start to reject negativity, feeling very uncomfortable under negative situations, you can't even watch the news, rejecting seeing negativity on social media posts, all your posts now are about love, laugh and positive content.
- You feel the energies around you and too many energies and crowded places make you feel uncomfortable, so you prefer the solitude at home.

- You feel the urge to help the environment, mother earth, and nature.
- You feel the necessity to help others, and friends and family are seeking your advice.
- You are very interested in learning more about self-healing, natural healing, and spiritual healing.
- You start to take care of your physical body by doing a vegetarian to vegan diet and attending Yoga classes.
- You start to mediate, and every time you do it's getting easier and feeling very comfortable and happy with a new calm mind.
- You start to feel positive towards life and you are a strong believer of the Law of Attraction, knowing that you can get what you want training your subconscious mind to be in the present moment feeling that you already have it.
- You feel a tremendous and unexplainable peace when you go to sleep at night, you feel that you are connected to the universe and you are very well protected by the spiritual realms while you sleep.
- You start to believe in self-healing, having the power to control your body, to regenerate and revitalize it with your mind and intentions.
- You have this special connection with animals, feeling their love, and want to protect them and be their voice.
- You want to spread the love, light, and happiness to others. You feel like you are a shining star, and your inner light can bright the earth in connection with the Universe.
- You respect life in all matters and forms, knowing that you are part of everything and everything is part of you.

So if you can relate to any of these statements, you definitely awaken your spirit, and now it's time for you to find your path in life.

What is your purpose in life? What are you here for? By the spirit, you will know and it will be downloaded into your being the information to continue with your spiritual journal.

The universe corresponds to your thinking and feeling, being Spiritual is the key for success in all areas in your life, you will be amazed on how you can control your life, how you can feel the oneness with the universe within you and all that it is.

Now you understand that everything is energy moving at different frequencies and speeds, and you are one of them, you are one with the divine. You now understand that in order to keep your energy frequency and ascend to high dimensions, you must stay in a positive, calm, healthy and happy state of mind.

There is nothing impossible now for you, you are taking control of your mind, body, and spirit. You have become what you had been created, the same image as God.

You are the manifestation of God on earth, you are part of the divine family and everything is within you. You now understand the eternity within you and the oneness of all.

You are now a free Spirit in a dimensional, parallel and never-ending universe that God created for you to explore, learn and teach.

Enjoy your privilege and journey to be in the present moment, the right moment, in a physical body experimenting all the sensations of the magnificent Creation for us to celebrate life!

LEARNING HOW TO LET GO.

"In the process of letting go, you will lose many things from the past, but you will find yourself."- Deepak Chopra

You have to be not afraid to let it go. Let go of the fear to live the reality of what you really want.

Accept the perfection of the universe. You have to accept that you live in a perfect universe, that you are really good already, and you are part of this amazing creation. It's all within yourself.

When the desire impulse strikes within you, and the feeling of what you want right now, makes you afraid of the outcome, then you are not going to get anywhere in life. So let the fears go with the flow, and let yourself be the light, having the deep feeling, that the universe, is taking care of your body and soul.

All it's perfect around you, and you really are all of that, the essence of the existence within the universe, it's in your hands.

If you listen on other people desires, of how they want you to live your own life, you are not taking action of your desires, and you are not growing your spirituality and follow your path in life.

You have the most powerful computer in the world, which is your brain in your physical human body, and when you produce any level of fear, you create a chemical reaction in your brain.

The brain has to convince itself, that if you feel fear that's a threat to your very survival and the only way you can break this up, is to say:

Forget it! I know it feels scary, but I am going all the way through it, and get what I want!

When we don't think we are not good enough for what we desire, we made conscious decisions; and that decisions can drastically changes our outcomes. So, this is why it's so important, to train our subconscious mind, to act in favor of our conscious mind.

You don't get what you want, you get what you feel you are. You are a true God Manifestation, the essence of who you are is perfect. You are a magnificent powerful creator, you have been through so much and you are still here, and that means you are good enough to get what you want and desire in your life. You have God within you. You are totally perfect spiritually.

SELF HYPNOSIS FOR SUCCESS.

"What if you create one sentence or question that's so loaded with hypnosis and assumptions that it totally blows out a person's problems?"–Igor Ledochowski

Creating sentences to be imprinted into your subconscious mind with whatever wish you want, are techniques you can use to hypnotize yourself to make success come to your life.

Get your daily journal, and find a special place that is comfortable to you, and start making your statements, writing what you want in the present tense.
Always start with: "I am so grateful now that………." and fill the space in blank with your wish.

As you get into the writing of your positive affirmations in the present tense, feel immersed, connected, and know that you already have it.

You can use this method for money, love, career. It will start to get your mind into a trance, and to become a pattern in your subconscious mind.

Brainwashing yourself or hypnotize yourself is to create a pattern plan. A good habit to get into hypnotizing yourself is while you do common things like cooking, cleaning, taking a shower, pick a phrase that you like a sentence in the present tense.

You have Sixty Five Thousand thoughts a day, so if you consciously installing the most conducting operating system that will help you induce yourself into a state of hyp-nosis, you will set your mind into auto pilot for success.

KNOWING YOUR SPIRITUAL DNA.

"Genes are like the story, and DNA is the language that the story is written in." Sam Kean

As a creator you are manifesting the story within yourself, you have the power to interfere on how your story goes from now on, and when you let that story flow around you; and with unconditional love, you're creating a stream of light that spreads around others changing many stories and affecting the oneness DNA of all that exists.

When you start getting more attention to your spiritual DNA you connect with the divine source that serves all of us. The more awareness that you are whole and divine, and you are made of love and light, then you are shifting your awareness of the truth of who you really are.

Who you are is perfection, total abundance, love, freedom and perfect health. Get appreciation of your true self, serve the knowledge of your spirituality and listen to your inner self and spiritual guides. Do not focus on your human cells, focus on your divine cells. The essence of who you are, is perfect.

When you start to give attention to that, you see things opening it up for you. Start focusing on your true nature, connect to your spiritual DNA. Your spiritual DNA is perfect!

Tap into those energies, feel the power within you that you are all what it is and you can transform your cells and spiritual DNA into that wealth and abundance frequency.

You have the unlimited power inherited from generations of spiritual divine beings, trillions of cells functioning at the same time that you were about to conceive, the right moment when your parents made you, that moment was sacred harmonized and transmuted into a form of 3D reality for you to be able to experience life on earth.

So now, you are here on earth with a purpose, you have all the power, the sacred knowledge, the spiritual awareness that you can tap into it anytime you wish, because now you can feel that there is more than this earth experience. You can bring those spiritual energies into your life now and transform it into something majestically arranged by you and what do you wish.

There is not stopping on learning, there is not stopping on knowing how powerful you are, you are discovering in a daily basis, how you can live and create your dreams. You are now stepping into this high frequency of love, happiness, abundance, and perfect health; because you are perfection. You were created as the same image of God, Source of Universe of the creation itself.

Know your worth, you are worthy of everything of what you desire, and now is the time to acclaim your power, to possess the riches you rightfully deserve, and experience life in the highest deeper level that you couldn't even imagine before.

Brake all those barriers from the past, let it go, it doesn't serve you anymore, feel how they leave your body and they float away from you in the deepest levels of the universe, healing and transformed into an experience learned, and express your soul now of who you truly are, you are a divine being in a third dimensional body, to live and manifest your experience on earth.

So tap into the higher frequencies of your spiritual realm and bring those energies to your present moment, to the essence of your being in the connection of the center of the universe, the power source, and everything that spin and circulates around it, in the same frequencies to create the life you want Now!

EVERYTHING ALREADY EXISTS.

"Without deep reflection one knows from daily life that one exists for other people." Albert Einstein

There are many infinite realities and outcomes that they are happening at the same time. We live in a spiritual dimensional and illusionary world. You are at the control and you get to decide which one you want to be part of it.

As you are a spiritual being, you have the ability to direct your consciousness, in the direction you want. You can harness conscious images and the power of the universe to send the frequencies out into the field to get into the vibrational frequencies of what you want.

Every time you have a tough, and you get emotionally involved in it, feeling that you already have it, and it's already happening; you're sending this energy field to the universe. It's like you are broadcasting yourself into what you want, and you're creating a consciousness simulation. So, based on the dominant energy that you are sending out, is the energy field you will get in return.

Most people in this world, live in a brainwashed consciousness. You have the ability to think, the way you want to think. Sending your electrical vibrational thinking, into the nervous system on how you want to feel.

All potential outcomes already exists. You get to decide what realities you want to live. You can create an amazing outcome for yourself. Create what you really want! Create freedom!

Liberate yourself from overthinking, consider that the power of your thoughts, the action and reaction are doing right now in your life. You have been programed on your early age, on what society wants you to be.

But, what do you want to be? You have the power to believe, and be, on what you want to be, and believe. You have the control of your own life.

Realities have created the situations, so be careful with your thoughts.

LEARNING FROM NATURE.

"Look deep into nature, and then you will understand everything better." Albert Einstein

Nature is the greatest teacher to take the time to nurture your spirit and connect with the Universe.

Flowers, grasses trees and vegetables; they land on earth to create beauty, for all living things.

Creation is perfect, all living things are connected, and nature is nurturing and teaching itself to the oneness of all, the perfection and beauty, that nature brings into our bodies, mind and spirit.

By taking care of our lives again it is understanding that everything has a purpose in the natural state. Our lives are connected. We need to take plants seriously, they are the keepers of the earth, they are the essence of our existence, our oxygen and food to our mind, body and soul.

Everything has a life, and everything interact with one and another. There is an association of everything.

A RELATIONSHIP TO KEEP INTACT.

"Love yourself. Enough to take the actions required for your happiness. Enough to cut yourself loose from the drama-filled past. Enough to set a high standard for relationships. Enough to feed your mind and body in a healthy manner. Enough to forgive yourself. Enough to move on." – Steve Maraboli

There is a relationship of love and kindness with all the creation. There is value, when you want to grow your own thoughts, when you connect with nature, the universe, and all that exists.

Live in harmony, listen to the wisdom of nature and connect with all what it is, and all the creation.

Develop a relationship with yourself, speak to yourself.

What do you really want? Think of the health of your emotions. Are they healthy? Are your emotions make you feel good? Do you feel complete? In the right state of mind?

Determined to regain and claim what was taking away from you.

Interconnection and support with each other in conjunction with your well being, is the goal for an enlightenment on earth, and to finally reach peace.

Look into your life skills, jobs skills. What does make you feel plenty? What does it makes you feel happy? Learn and seek for more, never stop, never give up!

Your powerful mind, can attract what you really want in life, use your skills to get into the state of unconscious mind, and finally hit the spot, and choose the reality you want to be into.

HOW TO ATTRACT MIRACLES.

"Give yourself a gift of five minutes of contemplation in awe of everything you see around you. Go outside and turn your attention to the many miracles around you. This five-minute-a-day regimen of appreciation and gratitude will help you to focus your life in awe."_ Wayne Dyer

We all have the ability to attract miracles. Forget about that phrase "This is always happening to me". The meaning you give the event, is the belief that cause it.

The energy you put into your belief is what caused and attracted it in the first place. Question your believe, because it's not the reality, it's not a fact.

As long as you are resisting them, you are keeping alive, because of the energy you are putting into them. All the belief that is within you.

Knowing what you don't want and taking control of it, is setting an intention of what you want. Get a clear idea of your desires, and rewire your beliefs. Train yourself to find blessings on everything. Let go of what is taking your inspired action, do not get the energy of desperation overwhelm you. Let love be your religion, and surround yourself with positive affirmations, people and good energies.

There is an energy that comes with an idea, so when you get an idea, is when you need to act fast, write that energy out to create that idea.

BREAKING THE NEGATIVE ENERGY CYCLE.

"Don't live the same day over and over again and call that a life. Life is about evolving mentally, spiritually, and emotionally." Germany Kent

Breaking the automatic pilot action. What is the trigger that cause you act like that? What do you see yourself? What do you feel? What do you hear?

It is time to create a peace in your environment. Bringing light to your behavior is an awareness, knowing that positive energies will boost your personal confidence. And the next time this happens to you, implement your strategies.

The main thing is to keep the fun. The beginner of your ideas and strategies will be to have a fulfilling happy and fun life. So create your life and toughest around those feelings, and you can never go wrong.

HIGHLY SUCCESSFUL PEOPLE SECRETS.

"We can't solve problems by using the same kind of thinking we used when we created them." — Albert Einstein

Perseverance, never give up. One more time, one more presentation, one more request, and you can achieve a lot more. Whatever you dreams is, do not give up.

Write twenty things that you like to do, and then decide, what is the job that will make you happy doing what you want to?

Take responsibility, do not blame other people for your experiences. You are full responsible of what you think, visualize and control your experiences.

Beliefs are like the color lens you're looking trough. Everything you look at, has a shade. When you beliefs are beginning to shift, and think that anything is possible, something happens in your life, you get an Aha! moment, and the moment you change your belief, you upgrade your life.

Be clear with yourself about what you believe and what you want to change. There are many ways to find your passion, strengths and inner-talents. Play your part in the battle of your own life, as well as the uplifter of humanity.

We are energy moving in a high speed vibration, and knowing that ninety five percent of an atom it's an empty space, the spirit it's what manifest the physical world.

Your energy creates the physical reality. You have the actual control and domain where your lives go. Everything is energy, your thoughts creates reality.

Lack of evidence is not evidence of lack. If you don't see or feel something, it doesn't mean that it doesn't exist.

Everything what you want already exists. You are a spiritual being in a physical body. Spirit it what it gives life to this world.

Close your eyes and imagine the world you want to live in. Every time you do that, you brain starts firing and accepting that reality as real brain can wire to a reality that doesn't exist. You can mold, shape and change your entire life however you want.

Start affirming of what you want is already here, it's coming, you can feel it, you are so grateful to the universe.

Do not desperate, every time you come from that kind of energy, it only breeds more or that desperation; and that energy moves to a place that is not powerful.

We were conditioned by society to believe that we live in a physical world, that we are separated from things we want. Every single thing you want is energy. All the things we see, they are different frequencies, vibrations and speed.

You have the propensity to believe that something outside of you, will fix the problem, but doing this, only enhances and magnifies the existing problem, and what happens is, you lose your power.

You have all what you need, to create the life that you want. You are connected to everything of what you want, you are not separate, and when you realize this frequency, you start to understand, that you are the consciousness that creates everything.

All the abundance that you desire, already exists for you. There is nothing you need to fix; you need to express the perfection within you.

To be in the alignment of what you want, you must feel good, to enhance your vibration on the deeply subconscious level, to bring what you want into your experience much quicker.

Start using the words "please" and "thank you" more in your life. When we do this, we align with gratitude, and feeling good, by giving gratitude to our surroundings.

Gratitude is truly the foundation of the Law of Attraction, in a more powerful way. When we are in deeper alignment with gratitude, you feel more powerful, and with the good feeling of attracting what you want, you'll be in harmony of what you're attracting.

Respect mother earth is respect our physical bodies. Picking up the trash you see on the streets, on the beach, on the park. You're deep-ling your surroundings and yourself in a higher way, and it's absolutely incredible! That's the type of energy that makes you feel amazing! Respect mother earth, respect it by taking this opportunity to clean up, to align with the essence of everything.

Smiling is literally imprinting into your system the feeling good sensation. There is nothing in this world that's aligns with love, than sharing a smile. It's a way to create connection to yourself, others and it feels amazing and good! Be an amplified energy of happiness!

Respecting your surroundings: do small task of kindness and offering others the services. Make someone else's job easier. Respect will start showing up in all your areas.

If you see a penny on the floor, pick it up! Do not walk over it, it's worth something. When you see a sign of abundance, say thank you, pick it up. You must start recognizing when signs are coming. "Thank you universe for showing me abundance."

There are infinite realities. There is a reality that you can't see, strictly because the way your consciousness has been conditioned, and you live in the exact opposite reality. Just think that everything are picture frames, and the world is movie frame. Your consciousness, is a projector that flashes different frames on your life. Everything is energy, you create your own energy.

You have the free will to decide in the reality you want to enter. Everyone energy field has a certain bandwidth in it. Start looking at the way you perceive reality. All the riches and happiness in the world, are really within you.

Explore your thoughts, explore your belief system around abundance. You've been conditioned by society to believe and make you feel that you are not enough to make money, with limited thoughts.

So, it is time for you to start to break free from that vicious circle that doesn't get you anywhere in life. And we do this by training yourself to be in the positive alpha and omega of our existence. We rewire our brain with fresh and crispy ideas of what our life should be.

TO BE OR NOT TO BE IN THE PRESENT TIME.

"Learn to focus only on the present. The past is unchangeable so it is futile to reflect on it unless you are making sure you do not repeat mistakes. The future is but a result of your action today. So learn from the past to do better in the present so that you can succeed in the future."_ Jordan Lejuwaan

Knowing that the past is gone, and the future is not here yet. We can realize that all we have left is the present. Staying focused in the present, and knowing that everything that we want is already created, will bring healing to the past, consciousness in the present, and a bright new beginning. And if we start feeling good now, every second that passes, will be our past, creating the reality of the present to attract what we want in the future.

The best way to train our subconscious mind, is to create our reality with positive affirmations in the present tense. So get your journal, and start writing how you want your life to be. Make a movie in your mind, of how do you want it to happen, make each frame unique, and be the author, the editor, the actor, the viewer and critic at the same time.

Enjoy the journey! be creative, start changing your life now! You have the knowledge, the key and the power to get everything you want. Life is yours, and your reality it's within you, in your hands.

You were created as the same image as God, so you are love, light and powerful creating energy! Take back your power! Take back what really belongs to you!

VISUALIZE YOURSELF INTO
THE REALITIES THAT YOU WANT TO CREATE.

"You are more productive by doing fifteen minutes of visualization than from sixteen hours of hard labor." Abraham Hicks

Focus on end situations, as if they already occur. Imagine yourself into these realities before it's already happening.

Congratulate yourself! When you do that, your brain starts thinking that already happened, because it doesn't know the difference between what is real or unreal.

The universe doesn't understand language, the universe understand frequency and feelings. How you feel will create the necessary energy frequency to manifest what you want into your present reality.

Be creative, imagine every single detail, circumstance and anything you want in it. When you start implanting this way of thinking and feeling, your life will start to change drastically and the right opportunities will start appearing into your life like Magic!.

Brainwash yourself, before the world brainwashes you. Download divine love, download blessings from the realm infinite possibilities, download the inspiration, creativity and ideas of what you need. Become clear, let go of what you need to let go.

Cleanse your energies, so you can be present, centered and opened. Your vibration will lift into the light, love and frequencies of inspiration that is available to you in the present moment.

At some point is going to be a clear download that is going to create. Stepping in of doing your work, complete your mission. Surround yourself with the light, open up, to receive the frequencies of light and healing love that is available to you now; your high divine true.

Act unto your inner inspiration to let the opportunities, and aloud a higher light to heal and flow into your body, mind and spirit.

The profound healing energy is available. Find your space into your inner self, and find that divine peace and feel who you really are. Trust and know, that you align with a higher lever of your divine. You acting on your creative inspiration, Ignore the doubt take action, to live your high vibration light. Quiet your mind and tune into the love, to expand and increase your radiance of love and light.

Opening your doorway to the energy to get your inner child back, listening to your energy and love. Making yourself the priority, align embracing your creativity. Align with your higher possible timeline. Align with the higher true of what is possible to you.

Remember deep down that everything is going to be okay. The best is about to be, stay focus on the highest intentions of what you really want, your inner light, your clear energy. All is possible to you to create, it's time to receive the inspiration, and coupling into your life.

Repeat to your mind: Floods of financial freedom opening up in my life... Large sums of money comes to me easily as I earn…....   Using a repetition, it will start opening the flood gates, and money will start coming to you easily.

Large sums of money comes to me easily as I earn…....
Engage your brain cells, practice visualizing end results. Imagine your boss shaking your hand, your dream home. End results will trigger your subconscious mind of what you want it's already happening.

TRUST THE PROCESS.

Hold the Vision. Drop the excuses. Remember your why. Swerve around obstacles. Trust the process. Happiness and success will find you. – Karen Salmansohn

Do not worry about how you will get into it. Affirm the prosperity. Start focus on prosperity, look for it prosperity. Your life can change instantly and flood of blessings will start to showing. Great things are happening in your logical mind.

Find a comfortable place where you can detach from the physical world. Tune into the love and presence, relax your mind, find your place between your toughs. Enter into your inner world. Enter deep into your heart center, in the divine I am presence, into that place letting your mind flows a golden energy, and accepting your mind activation to receive the energy, to raise up above, until you tune into love and light.

Tune into it, let the light and let yourself deep into it. And begin to expand that light, the blessings of love and frequencies of healing, and knowing your higher self.

Receive the guidance, just be open to receive and connect with all what it is. You have this ability to direct, connect, and tune into the guidance of your divine true. Tune into the higher positive energy all around you, supporting you, and guiding you, of who you can be.

CREATE A VISION BOARD.

Vision without action is merely a dream. Vision with action can change the world. -Joel A Barker

Having a vision board it's so essential to start to create and vision the life you want to create.
I
This in alignment of creating of what you want. We can create that, in our imagination, but creating the vision board, gives you instant gratification, because you are able to see, what is in your mind.

It is a extremely powerful way to set that reminder in your brain. It's been in alignment to raise your vibration.

While you creating your vision board, do not judge yourself. Just be in the experience and joy of it. It is a moment of inspiration, creating something that is creating joy.

Create a board that just bring happiness, that cultivate joy within you.

Create a vision, and a language, to your vision world. Calling, remind it, of what you want: a home, travel, exercise; inspiring things that makes you feel good.

Creating a vision, board is another way to manifest, of what you are becoming, connecting to a deep level of creating your reality. Create all those amazing dreams you want to accomplish.

USING MEDITATION TO CREATE
A SUPER NATURAL MIND.

"Empty your mind, be formless, shapeless – like water. Now you put water into a cup, it becomes the cup, you put water into a bottle, it becomes the bottle, you put it in a teapot, it becomes the teapot. Now water can flow or it can crash. Be water, my friend." Bruce Lee

Subjecting changes, produce subjecting objecting results in the external world. How do you make these changes?

Anything that is repeatable. Consider well being as a skill. Cope with diversity, how we respond to diversity, is the key to well being. Have the ability, to naturally learn to become and recover quickly from any negative event.

Everything we do, will affect our brain, the way we confront ourselves will affect our brain. Our brain will change because our mental habits. The way to change this habits, is with meditation practice.

Raising your energy in your body, you are responsible for reducing suffering in this world.

Inner revolution is happening now, these can be transforming and create the best being you can possible be. The resting mind will use a baseline.

Being spiritual and in a sense of connection of something higher than yourself.

Overwhelming state of love, feeling connected with abundance. When you truly presence you forget about time and space. You are not distracted by anything.

Getting yourself beyond the identity of a body it is a skill. The same level of mind, that you have living every day, is not the mind, that is going to produce transformation; you have to transcend your inner world, and loose track of time.

When we drop into meditation we drop the body. The mind is telling us, come this way.

HOW TO DESTROY UNCONSCIOUS BLOCKAGES AND NEGATIVITY.

"There's a way that you can throw negativity out there that seems rebellious. But I've always taken pleasure in a different kind of rebellion, which is putting a positive spin on everything, trying to enjoy myself at all times."- Zac Efron

Destroying your unconscious blockages and negativity starts within you, allowing yourself to wake up your spiritual gifts, who you really are: You were created as same image as God, so you are love, light and creative energy.

Creating is your birthright as a spiritual being in a human form. Aligning all your energies into the core of your soul, to recognize the power that lives within you. A power that you can use anytime you wish. This power is the creative energy within you. You can create many realities and choose which reality, you want to tune into it.

Pushing yourself beyond your ego, which is telling you cannot. Following your heart desires and intuition to manifest your magnificent creative potential and your ideas bringing them into existence.

Your Joy, Love, and Faith act as a guidance system in life, aligning you with your creative mind, to expand and reproduce tons of toughs that will carry strong creative energy that comes from your spiritual essence which is divine.

HOW TO LET GO AND FEEL FREE.

"Let go of the battle. Breathe quietly and let it be. Let your body relax and your heart soften. Open to whatever you experience without fighting." -Jack Kornfield

Letting go is clearing and shield your energy into the deepest spiritual recognition. As you advance in your spirituality you will become sensitive to the density of toxicity and negativity, compared to the reality of higher dimensions of love.

Taking action of clearing and elevating your energetic space. Breathing into the light of who you really are. You are divine light and love, receiving the blessings of healing frequency. Feeling the love from inside of you, replenishing your body moving you into the direction of peace, love, joy, and freedom.

Breathe naturally, feeling the white bright light clearing and releasing the dense energy, toxic patterns, negativity, and limited beliefs which no longer serves you.

Imagine this beautiful light shining all around you, feel the Christ energy: peace, love, joy; and know that you can call this beautiful light anytime to cleanse, uplift, and protect you in all levels.

Setting your intention clear, breathing into the light, knowing that this divine gift, is available for you at all times to shield you from what no longer serves you, and bringing peace, love, joy and freedom; assisting you in lifting into a new level of vibrant well being.

WHAT SYNCS TOGETHER LINKS TOGETHER.

"It is during our darkest moments that we must focus to see the light." Aristotle Onassis

Opening your focus and sense space and nothing the long that you can be there, in the wholeness your brain will become to be more integrating. In the alpha, all of the sudden, the inner world becomes to be, in the outer world. The right side of the brain, talks to the left side of the brain; that energy goes right into the heart, and the person start feeling connected to something greater.

Stepping into the practical, changing your original state. What happens internally when the energy hits your being, you can feel the light, the movement. Your inner experience is greater, your connection with the divine; everything around you is love, unconditional love.

Switch into the energies of the unknown, is certainly is a way, to conquer your subconscious mind, to be in the flow in the present time. Let yourself go wild, in the deep sense of spirituality, let your inner self grow into the collective consciousness of all what it is.

In everything of what you do, feel or think is arranged, in proportion of your desires, and outcomes. So be careful of the message you are sending to the world, you are like a mirror, that reflect yourself, in the deep level of consciousness with the higher realms of the universe itself. You are one with the oneness, and everything is you, and about you.

More deep into your thoughts, there are many resources of many outcomes. Choose wisely what you want to create, counting your blessings in proportion of your desires, aligning yourself with the infinite abundance of your royal heritage, because you are the higher consciousness of your being and spirit in proportion with the rest of what is created, at the same rhythm of the universe. With the allowance of your thoughts, become the reality, you wish to happen in your life.

You have the command, you are the captain of your life, and you move into the direction you wish to experience, with a life full of infinite possibilities, that are all exists in the present moment.

Your life is about to change, you have the power to survive your fears, you have the power to acknowledge the right direction, and certainly make the right decisions based on your connection with inner self.

Your spiritual realms are connected to the infinite universe, that it's extending the countless, endless, and infinite possibilities, of overcome obstacles, and turning them into the experience, of letting get behind our conscious mind, surviving our existence, in a deep level of gratitude, towards the essence of our inner spiritual base, leading our subconscious mind to reciprocate the feelings and thoughts into something tangible and real.

Many of us, are unrealistic of the many resources in existence to procreate within our mind a successful life, and we blame outside and out-world circumstances, as the effect that is producing our low self esteem, to be the leader of or non coexistence, with all what it is.

The universe itself, is programing and downloading, the information we need, to perceive the many possibilities, that are around us, in the present moment, in another dimensions, but with a conscious frequency of the dimension we want to experience; we can bring it into reality.

CONNECTING WITH OTHERS
AND HARMONIZING RELATIONSHIPS

"The best and most beautiful things in the world cannot be seen or even heard, but must be felt with the heart."
—Helen Keller

Connecting with others and starting amazing relationships, it always starts with yourself first. You are love, you were created in the same image as God, so you're love, light, and energy. Taking your power back in Love, Joy, and Faith; the Christmas Spirit, the Christ energy, that's the energy frequency that you need to be every single day of your life, to have an amazing life experience.

Healing your Body, Mind, and Spirit with this beautiful energy frequency, being in the present moment, letting go of the past, and don't worry about the future.

When you live in the present moment with Love, Joy, and Faith, you healed the past, and create a wonderful future.

So when you understand this concept that loves comes within you first, then you're ready to have a meaningful connections with others and harmonizing your relationships.

It is also in the Bible: "The Kingdom of Heaven is Within You". The energy that you put within yourself, is what you spread to the Universe, and then the Universe will bring that back that energy multiplied in many blessings.

The thought patterns and limiting beliefs that keep you being in a beautiful relationship, are nothing more than mental habits.

You can dismantle those habits and create new neural pathways that will enable you to let go of the drama, stay away from toxic people and keep your mind focus in Love, Joy, and Faith will bring the peace that you desire and deserve, your Mind, Body and Spirit will be at ease, to connect with others who are at your same frequency, at your same spiritual level.

You really let yourself be in and let go of old ideas of how society has programing you to be. When you unconsciously resist your ability to create harmony in your relationships, you are creating your own blockages that is impeding this relationship to succeed. This can of action creates tension, but it can be eliminated once you consciously move into the energy of acceptance, Love, Joy, and Faith.

Actually, you don't need anyone to feel love because you're love. If you choose to be with someone, accept them as they are and not the version you wish them to be. You are sharing your love with this person, you don't need them to feel love, and they don't also need you. Allow them to grow and transform at their own pace and continually choose to accept them exactly as they are in each moment; because you are adjusting to each other. A relationship is a contract of sharing your love together and adjusting to each others energies.

When embracing compassion, love, faith, and kindness you'll find that your connection will naturally be deeper as these energies are rooted in trust and kindness. With the Christ energy in mind, you choose love over jumping to nonsense conclusions or assuming other things. The desires of compassion, kindness, and harmony embrace love.

Choosing love over fears and doubts will come from a place of compassion and gentleness. This is how you choose harmony over drama.

When you are in a relationship, do not forget about taking care of yourself. Never put your partner in a pedestal, that's your place because as we said before love comes from you and within you, then putting someone else on a pedestal, is a lack of self-love. You really always need to work on your own personal growth. You need your own space-time to breathe, expand, and meditate. Your partner also needs the same.

You are not competing with each other, you are completing each other, two beautiful souls choosing come together in the name of Love, Joy, and Faith.

RECOGNIZING A TWIN FLAME CONNECTION

"Twin flames have an instant, instinctive and undeniably intense bond. As soon as they meet, they feel an overwhelming and familiar "home" sensation, as though they have known one another before." -Alex Myles

When you meet your twin flame you have an instant and intuitive feeling of connection of being at home, you feel safe and you know this is the One.

As saying One, this twin flame connection is One with you, feeling that this connection have been brought you together as part of a divine plan, a higher calling, you feel not only a physical connection but also spiritual.

At the beginning of the relationship of a twin flame connection, it might be a little hard to deal with, as you both are working in reunite and merge your energies and balanced as one.

Twin flames are powerful but if one of you are not in the frequency of Love, Joy and Faith, then can be very dramatic. One of you is the higher Spirit and one of you must keep the good energy within him until the other twin reach the spiritual level of the One.

When the One fall into the other negative energy can cause separation, but it will be for a short time to heal and recuperate and adjust the energies again. This connection of shared energies will always keep you linked regardless of the physical space, you always be connected .

When the adjustment of energies is made and the spiritual connection will be at the same level, twin flames will experience the most loving, amazing partnership, with a deep connection emotionally, mentally, physically and spiritually.

The purpose of the twin flame is to balance each other in a perfect, harmonious amazing relationship. This is the Ying Yang of the Twin flame connection, adjusting and balancing each other until reach stability.

A twin flame connection needs more than a physical attraction, there is an intense exchange of energy, it's about respect.

The physical connection is not based only in sexual attraction, if sexual contact occurs, the important nature of this connection is two souls that are communicating with their bodies.

Then we have the spiritual connection, which is the ability to sense each other's emotions, even if you're miles apart, and this is a sign when twin flames are connected. It's a beautiful and sacred state of unconditional love created from the capacity of each one to let go of their ego and connect with each other with tenderness and loving care.

Once this harmony has occurred, twin flames will begin vibrating on the same frequency and experience a union of unconditional love.

WHO IS GOD?

God is to me that creative force, behind and in the universe, who manifests Himself as energy, as life, as order, as beauty, as thought, as conscience, as love.- Henry Sloane Coffin

There is an infinite presence, eternal, divine intelligence that is everything. Every cell of your body, every atom is this divine energy is the physical assumption of your spiritual divine energy.

You allowing your spiritual essence to consume in a deeper level of the whole existence, and how to manifest God in your life, is how you are responding to your spiritual DNA of who you are really are. You are all and everything of your-existence, and when you accept that in your life, as a true divine fact, the magic of God start showing in your life.

We live in a physical Universe with physical forms. What we think we can perceive with our naked eye, is our reality, and we live with this unexplainable side phenomena that was cause by physicals matter is wrong. Albert Einstein told us that energy and matter are the same thing.

All physical things are made of atoms and atoms are 99.99% empty space. So we have the power to control were the energy goes, we can create and transform energy; we have into our Spiritual DNA this God's energy; because we are one with God, one energy and everything is one within us.

Our divine energy frequency is vibrating basically at such as pure frequency of light, that we can't see all of it, 99.99% of your body, the chair you sit on, your car is empty space; is divine light, is divine consciousness, it's God, it's spirit vibrating at a frequency, that is outside of the spectrum, of visible light that your eyes can't see.

God is this source of energy that is never created or destroyed, infinite light of wisdom, multiplied in many light forms and at the same time, connected to each other, moving at different frequencies and that is what it's creates its physical form.

Every cell of your body, has this pure frequency of God, you are in pure control of your emotions to manifest God's energy flow within you, and manifest what you want in the physical form, and this is exactly what it is God's creative energy.

AFFIRMATIONS TO ATTRACT ABUNDANCE.

I deserve abundance, I expect miracles.

I expect to have all the abundance in this world!

New beginnings are coming Now! The rest of my life, will be the best of my life!

Money comes to me in increasing quantities, through many sources, on a continuous basis.

I receive the abundance of God, life is good.

All things work for my good, I'm blessed with constant miracles.

Today is the start of amazing things entering my life. I am so grateful.

I always keep moving forward.

I always think positive.

I accept, and love myself, for who I am.

Abundance surrounds me, I am very blessed.

Money flows to me, regardless of where I am.

I know how to create, many sources of income.

I believe that money is important, I love money!

Miracles and magic surrounds me everywhere I go.

Thank you Universe!, I have everything I need.

Thank you Universe, my life is filled with success and richness.

I am worthy of all of what I desire.

I rejoice of being a millionaire.

I feel proud of myself.

I allowed myself to feel, and be successful.

I celebrate life, love, and abundance everyday.

Thank you universe, for the constant blessings I'm receiving everyday

I trust and follow my inner guts.

Thank you Universe, my finances increases everyday.

I rejoice of being a millionaire.

Thank you universe!, I have a constant supply of money.

I deserve to make millions of dollars.

I am motivated to make large amount of money.

The universe is taking good care of me.

I am the designer and the creator of my own life. I trust my imagination.

Thank you universe, everything synchronizes perfectly, allowing me to make tons of money.

I am an excellent receiver.

Love is the connection, to all sources of income.

I am thankful for the small, and big blessings in my life.

I give thanks to prosperity.

Thank you universe, I feel energized, happier and younger everyday.

I becoming all that I can be.

Love is my inner experience, that reflect my outside life.

I am living a full complete life.

I am success and allowed myself to feel success.

Becoming a millionaire is something I will do naturally.

The mentality that I put into the world, reflects the outcome I am receiving into my life.

It is very easy for me, to make millions of dollars.

I attract the right people and circumstances to bring abundance and happiness into my life.

I am a winner, I play the life game to win!

Thank you universe, for responding to my intentions.

My inner world, creates my outer.

My thoughts and feelings, are proportional, to the abundance, I am receiving.

I am with the infinite riches of my subconscious mind.

I create the reality, that I wish to be in.

My endless supply of money, it is created from my subconscious mind.

I communicate clearly, and professionally.

The feelings that I put into my toughs, creates the success and abundance in my life.

I think positive, therefore I am positive.

I like what I am.

I am success and allowed myself to feel success

Believing, loving, and trusting in myself, is the key to create the amazing world I am in!

My intentions are to create, wealth and abundance.

My inner self, is defying my outer world.

I celebrate life, training my mind, to be in the perfect state of consciousness, in the present time.

Money is energy, I manifest and draw that energy.

I committed to be rich.

I am surrounded by the most powerful spiritual beings, that are helping to follow my right path experience.

I create the abundance that I wish to live in.

Everything is proportional to my thoughts and feelings.

Positive outcomes are always following me.

Having a proportional thoughts and feelings, creates a steady abundant and proportional life.

I live in unlimited abundance.

I have the ability to attract millions of dollars.

I have more money than I ever dreamed possible.

I live in abundance.

I am creating unlimited wealth.

Today is a good day, to make a fortune.

It is my right to be rich, happy, and successful.

I give thanks, that I am rich.

I'm the builder of my life.

I become rich, by giving value to other people's lives.

I am a strong money maker.

I love money, and money loves me back.

The Universe says YES to me.

I am happy, healthy and multi millionaire.

I construct wealth easily.

My prosperity prospers others.

I see myself living a life of abundance.

I notice prosperity all around.

I am know from my positive energy, and abundance.

I use money for good.

I associate myself, with wealth money people.

I attract prosperity with every thought.

Money is a source of good, for myself and others.

I render a wonderful service, in a wonderful way.

Money is always circulating in my life.

Each moment brings new opportunities.

I prosper in everything I do.

I vision complete abundance.

Money is my friend.

I know I deserve prosperity of all kinds.

My positive money thoughts are coming through.

Life is so easy, I trust that everything comes to me in a perfect time.

I believe anyone can be a millionaire, and that's include me.

I demonstrate love with action everyday.

I have faith that I've been guided in ways that brings amazing results.

My inner wisdom, guides me to make the right decisions.

I demonstrate love with actions everyday.

I have a positive mindset.

I am alert to opportunities.

I now create my wonderful ideal life.

I choose exactly what I want in life, developing consciousness with any choices.

My income automatically rises higher.

My bank account is always growing.

Money is good, money is energy, I am energy.

I invite and allow good, to come into my life.

I'm always in the right place, the right time.

Things I create are even better than I imagine them to be.

My income is always increasing.

My income is always rising.

My mind is tune to prosperity.

I now allow to my income to multiply.

I visualize financially abundance.

I believe that my prosperity is growing.

I have an abundant mindset.

I have a prosperity mindset.

I only focus in prosperity.

My income increase rapidly.

My financial situation is always improving.

I am now tuned to the frequency of money.

I visualize and receive checks coming through the mail.

I only visualize prosperity.

Money just seems to be drawn to me.

I am now re-programing my subconscious beliefs to only focus in prosperity.

I am one with the vibration of prosperity

I am now tune, with the frequency of love.

My income is always increasing.

I only visualize prosperity.

I only visualize abundance.

My income in constantly increasing.

Prosperity is my middle name.

The more money I give away, the more money I receive.

I give because I love to give.

I love taking bold actions to increase my prosperity.

My income increases now.

Prosperity is my natural state.

My income is always rising.

My mind is tune to prosperity.

I now allow, for my income, to be multiply.

I believe that my prosperity is growing.

My income increases rapidly.

My financial situation is always improving.

I have more money that I know what to do with it.

I am known as a prosperous individual.

I am a magnet for all things prospers.

My income in constantly increasing.

I attract the right people, circumstances that increases my income.

Prosperity is my natural state.

My mind is tune to prosperity.

I visualize a prosperous life.

I visualize financial abundance.

I always take actions that grow my prosperity.

Money is easy to obtain.

Money comes to me easily and frequently.

I'm always attracting money.

I receive money easily and frequently.

Money follows me.

Money is drawn to me easily.

I'm always finding money.

I'm always receiving money.

Money is easy to make.

Money is easy to attract.

Money is drawn to me, like a magnet.

I receive money easily, from my ideas.

I work smart, and I make easy money.

Money falls into my lap, easily and frequently.

I'm always receive hunches to earn money easily and frequently.

Money falls simply into my lap.

Money always finds me.

I make smart money decisions.

Prosperity and abundance surrounds me.

I attract prosperity with every tough.

I enjoy prosperity and shared freely with the world.

I spend money wisely.

I expect the best, and I'm getting it now.

I'm so grateful now, that I posses abundance.

I deserve to have financial abundance, in my life now.

My greatest good, is here for me now.

I am grateful for everything what I receive in life.

I love making money, and enjoy to have multiple streams of positive income.

I expect leverage abundance every day and every way.

I always get everything, for my greatest good.

I know that prosperity, is all around me.

All I have to do, is ask for abundance and allow it.

I am thankful, for the unlimited flow of good, into my life.

I know that the world is prosperous.

I have the power to attract money.

If others can be wealthy, so can I.

I attract money naturally.

My bank balance, is increasing everyday.

The universe, constantly supplies money to me.

I give thanks for the prosperity, which is mine.

I feel great joy providing for my family, and all those that I love.

Wealth and prosperity is circulating in my life.

Money and I, are friends.

I believe that more abundance is coming to me now.

I am deserving of abundance, no matter what.

I am successful in every way.

I respect my ability to create wealth.

All things I seek, are now seeking me.

I allow the universe, to bless me with great abundance Now.

The seeds of great wealth, are beside me.

Each day is filled, with endless expressions of abundance.

Today I expand the awareness of abundance, around me.

My life is prosperous.

I am debt free, and money comes to me easily everyday.

I am in a constant state of fulfillment.

I have more money that I can't ever dream.

Wealth comes to me, from many sources.

I am grateful to be wealthy.

I welcome abundance, into my life.

I

I am free, to accumulate wealth.

My wealth allows me, to do whatever I want.

I use money, to make the world, a better place.

I am grateful for my wealth.

I allow wealth to shine through me.

I prosper in my finances.

I welcome wealth, with open arms.

Everything I need in life, is mine.

I invite wealth, in my life.

Each day, my life is filled, with wonderful abundance.

I am growing spiritually, emotionally and financially.

I allow myself to have good things in life, and I am enjoy them.

I have skills to create access to bring money.

I give thanks, for my incredible prosperous life.

Great wealth is flowing to me, now.

Unexpected income, is flowing to me.

Wealth and prosperity, is circulating in my life.

I am more wealthy, than I never imagined.

I was born to be prosperous.

Abundance flows easily, when I relax and let it happen.

I love the idea, to have truly effortless abundance.

I will live an abundant life.

I define success my way, and I created.

I attract the highest wealth, prosperous and minded people to me.

My life is prosperous.

It is easy for me to create wealth.

Each day my life, is filled with the magic of abundance.

I am open to be wealthy.

I was wealthy yesterday, I am wealthy today, and I will be wealthy tomorrow.

The only limits to my abundance, is me.

I live life abundantly.

I was prosperous, I am prosperous, and I will always be prosperous.

Abundance and I, are One.

I love abundance and prosperity, and I am attracting them naturally

I am always positive towards wealth.

I am passionate about building wealth.

I vanish the past, and now live in a wealthy Now.

I deserve to be successful, and prosperous.

Creating wealth, is my second nature.

I create wealth, easy and effortlessly.

I love abundance, in all its beautiful forms.

I release all negative beliefs of money, and now I attract money.

My income is growing higher now.

Whatever I do is always ends in a massive wealth.

I will be productive and prosperous today.

I always have whatever I need.

Perfect abundance is my chosen reality.

I am free to do, whatever I wish to do.

Been wealthy, gives me joy, happiness and peace of mind.

Feeling joyful, attracts abundance.

Wealth is a positive expression, of divine energy.
I can easily imagine myself, having limitless abundance.

I am prosperous in everything I do.

I see myself as wealthy, and that's who I am.

I give thanks, that I am now rich, wealthy and happy.

I am thankful, for the abundance, and prosperity in my life.

Everything and everyone, prospers me now.

I love abundance and prosperity, and I am attracting it naturally.

I love abundance in all its beautiful forms.

All I have to do, is ask for abundance and allows it.

I can see abundance everywhere around me.

Abundance is my divine birth right.

I am wealthy, successful and I love it!

I am synchronized, with the energies of abundance.

I love the abundance that I create everyday.

I am embracing these precious moments, every moment is filled with infinite possibilities.

I am a loving soul in a human body. I have a purpose being here. I am connecting with my true purpose.

I am allowing myself to attract success in my terms.

I am deserving, I am attracting and creating success from my heart.

Success flows to me, naturally.

I am allowed myself, to be guided.

I choose to follow, the threads of joy.

I'm giving thanks, for all the abundance in my life.

I am enjoying the success, that is showing itself, in different forms.

I gratefully going after, of what I want in life.

I am living in a river of creativity, and magnificent ideas.

I take action, of my awesome ideas.

I am inspired to express, my ideas and toughs.

I am magnet to success, abundance, and prosperity.

I am using the flow of abundance in my life, to create abundance for others.

I love to create value, for other people.

I am a positive thinker.

I am successful in all areas of my life.

I am passionate about life.

Abundance is a choice, I am choosing abundance, because I can.

I am now choosing, to consciously reprogram myself, for my higher good.

Acceptance is the key to freedom, I have that key.

I am ready, I am free to choose success.

I am truly excited, for all the abundance, that it's on my way now.

I choose to receive, with gratitude.

I choose to give generously, and unconditionally.

I am always learning new ways that brings even more success.

I invite abundance and wealth, within my life now.

I am choosing to be happy, for what I already have in my life.

I have a gift, of free will.

I am proud to be a person, that follows my goals, dreams, and desires.

All that I seek, seeks me.

I am connected with my higher self, and my unique creativity.

My vibration, is my reality.

I am allowing abundance, to flow and circulate freely, through me.

The universal intelligence, is supporting me.

I am a soul, in a human body.

My vibration is my reality, my vibration is my life.

I am free, generous, compassionate.

I am a divine spark, of the universal light.

I am pure power, in human form.

Success flows to me naturally.

I choose to live from my heart.

LOVE AFFIRMATIONS.

I love myself.

I love myself more from the day before.

I am loving, kind, and compassionate; to myself.

I choose to have loving toughs, about myself.

I no longer live in fear, I love myself.

I love myself fully now.

I am love.

I am loved.

I am lovable.

I am full of love for myself, and for others.

I am seeing love, everywhere I look.

I see love, when I look at myself.

I love myself more everyday.

It is safe for me, to love myself.

It is safe for me, to respect myself.

It is safe for me, to forgive myself and others.

I am in the most magic loving relationship.

I am living now, with my twin flame, the one that I was born to travel this lifetime with.

I am experiencing such joy, such incredible happiness in my heart, so peaceful satisfaction in my loving relationship.

I am spending time with my love, sharing the deeps of our souls, connecting in profound and meaningful ways.

I absolutely love myself.

I believe in my abilities to succeed.

I genuinely love, my own company.

I celebrate myself.

I am proud, of who I am becoming.

I praise myself.

I am amazing.

My opinion of myself is the only thing that matters.

I love me.

I am grateful to be alive.

I am charming, charismatic, and loving.

I truly love and support myself.

No one in this world, can be me, and that's my super-power.

I'm gifted, talented, and brilliant.

I'm taking care of my body, my body is my temple.

I have an amazing personality.

I am a valuable person.

I love and enjoy, my own company.

I absolutely love myself.

I am here to fulfill my purpose, and it will be wonder-ful.

I speak words of love to myself.

I celebrate myself.

I deserve the best life has to offer.

I am here to do amazing things.

I'm grateful to be alive.

I'm strong, powerful, and amazing.

I truly love, and support myself.

I am uniquely amazing.

I can do anything I set my focus on.

I love being alive, and I value myself.

I can do what no one can.

I believe in my abilities to succeed.

I love and enjoy my own company.

I attract lastly and happy relationships, into my life.

I give love, and it is return to me, multiplied many forms.

My heart is always open.

Everywhere I go, I find love.

I am surrounded by love.

My thoughts are always loving.

Today I bless my being with infinite love.

Every day my love grows stronger.

I naturally attract, perfect relationships, into my life.

All the love I need, is within me.

Today I chose to be loved, and happy.

My relationships, are created in infinite.

I attract love easily, and effortlessly

Love is all around me.

I am a magnet to love.

The more love I give,the more love I receive.

Everything I do, is in the vibration of love.

I give unconditional love to everyone.

My heart is filled with love.

I am motivated.

I have the power to the most incredible things.

I deserve love, and I get it in abundance.

I am now ready to accept a happy and loving relationship.

I am free of negative thinking.

I have the power to change my life.

Today I choose to give love, and joy.

I trust myself, and my decisions.

Every day I feel more loving, and lovable.

I attract success, in all areas of my life.

My relationships are created, in infinite love.

I am a magnet to love.

The more love I give, the more love I receive.

My thoughts are always loving.

Today I bless my being with infinite love.

Every day my love grows strong.

My belief in love, opens my heart to receiving.

I deserve love, and I get it in abundance.

I'm attracting loving and caring people, into my life.

I attract healthy loving relationships.

I deserve to receive love in abundance.

I deserve a loving and caring partner.

I am thankful for the love that currently surrounds me.

I am thankful for the way I love, and accept myself.

I happily give, and receive love everyday.

I happily invite love into my life.

I open my heart to love, and know that I deserve it.

I open my mind to amazing relationship possibilities.

Whatever I go, I find love.

Whatever I go, I am love.

I attract people who treat me with respect.

I attract people who are honest and kind.

I am worthy to be deeply loved.

I am worthy of been cherish and adored.

I deserve to be showered with affection.

I deserve a kind and cared lover.

I am grateful to be open to love in its many forms.

I give myself permission to love.

I joyfully give myself to give and receive love.

I open my heart to love

I open my mind to make ways to an amazing relationship.

I welcome a loving partner into my life.

I welcome a nurturing relationship into my life.

I am grateful for how loving I am.

I am grateful for how loved I am.

I enjoy comfortable authentic relationships.

I enjoy sharing my true self with my partner.

I deserve to feel safe and secure in a relationship

I deserve to feel love and honored.

I am worthy of a fulfilling relationship.

I am worthy of love.

I love myself because I am worth of love.

Love is all around me.

Happiness is a state of Love.

When there is love, there is abundance.

Gratitude is the key to feel and receive infinite love.

"If you want to change your life, start with you now.
Look deep into your heart, open and expand that infinite love within you.
You are the master of your life."

Yoselem G. Pintos